Architektur der Unendlichkeit

Architecture of Infinity

Scheidegger & Spiess

Architektur der Unendlichkeit

Architecture of Infinity

A Film by Christoph Schaub
Produced by maximage

Mit / with Peter Zumthor, Peter Märkli, Álvaro Siza Vieira, James Turrell, Cristina Iglesias, Jojo Mayer

Scheidegger & Spiess

Der Film

Zeitlichkeit wohnt jedem Ding und Wesen inne und transzendiert, je nach Anschauung, ins Unendliche. Wie kann ein solches Phänomen in Bilder übersetzt werden? In seinem Film setzt Christoph Schaub in einer persönlichen Reise durch Zeit und Raum bei seiner Kindheit an, als seine Faszination für sakrale Bauwerke und sein Staunen über Anfang und Ende begannen. Gemeinsam mit den Architekten Peter Zumthor, Peter Märkli und Álvaro Siza Vieira, den Kunstschaffenden James Turrell und Cristina Iglesias und dem Schlagzeugvirtuosen Jojo Mayer ergründet Schaub die Magie sakraler Räume, deren Definition hier weit über kirchliche Bauten hinausgeht.

Architektur der Unendlichkeit sucht Spiritualität in Bau- und bildender Kunst, aber auch in der Natur und hebt sie über Denkgrenzen hinaus. Eine leicht schwebende Kamera lässt uns eintauchen in traumwandlerische Bilder, nimmt uns mit auf eine (be-)sinnliche Reise in räumliche Weiten, führt unseren Blick in die Unendlichkeit des Sternenhimmels und in die Tiefe des Meeres.

The film

Temporality and age are inherent in every object and creature and, depending on one's outlook, may transcend to infinity. How can this be imagined? What goes beyond it? The filmmaker Christoph Schaub starts his personal journey through time and space in his childhood, when his fascination with sacred buildings began – and his wonder at beginnings and ends. Together with the architects Peter Zumthor, Peter Märkli and Álvaro Siza Vieira, the artists James Turell and Cristina Iglesias, and drummer virtuoso Jojo Mayer, Schaub explores the magic of sacred spaces, defined here as far more than church buildings. Who owns spirituality? The film follows "spiritual life" in architecture and the fine arts, but also in nature, and literally lifts it over and above the limits of thinking. A slightly floating camera immerses us in somnambulistic images, takes us on a sensual and sensing journey through vast spaces, and guides our eye towards the infinity of the starry sky and the depths of the ocean. Past and present, primeval times and light years, it's all there.

Sprechende Räume.

Christoph Schaubs *Architektur der Unendlichkeit*

Friedhelm Mennekes

Friedhelm Mennekes ist ein katholischer Theologe, Priester und Kunstverständiger. Er hat zahlreiche Bücher zu Fragen der Religion und der Kunst verfasst.

Künstler wie Eduardo Chillida (1924–2002) unterscheiden einen geometrischen Raum von einem künstlerischen. Dieser letztere sei genau das, was der Mensch brauche, um sich selbst zu finden und zu entwerfen. Jeder Mensch muss ihn für sich gestalten, erbauen und einrichten. Dieser künstlerische Raum ist zunächst ein Ort, an dem sich bestimmte Dinge einfinden; dies sind die Volumina, die Wände und Gegenstände, die einen solchen Raum abstecken. Zwischen ihnen und in ihnen ist Leere. Die formale Bestimmung des Raums wird inhaltlich durch das Handeln des Menschen geklärt, nämlich den ambitionierten Umgang mit ihm.

Von dieser Art künstlerischen Raums unterscheidet sich der sakrale Raum. Er ist der heilige Ort der Einkehr und anders als der künstlerische Raum. Drei seiner Dimensionen seien auf seine Funktionen hin angesprochen: er «ent-rückt», er sammelt und er erregt. Der Mensch braucht solche Orte, die die Möglichkeit eröffnen, aus dem akustischen und optischen Lärm hinaustreten zu können – hinein in einen Raum, in welchem Schweigen herrscht und wirkliches Hören und Innenerfahrung möglich wird. Hier zieht sich der Mensch in schweigender Sammlung nach innen zurück und grenzt sich nach aussen ab.

In seinem neuen Film über sakrale Räume geht Christoph Schaub von einem breiteren Begriff von Architektur aus. Er sucht sie vor allem von ihrer Wirkung her zu verstehen, von der Faszination, die Kirchen auf

ihn ausüben. Diese ziehen ihn an und interessieren ihn emotional, weil sie ihn persönlich ansprechen.

Der Mensch, der eine Kirche betritt, will zur Ruhe kommen. Seine Stimmungen sollten ausschwingen und dann von der Atmosphäre des Raums aufgefangen werden. Der Besucher sucht zunächst sich selbst, seine Geschichte, seine Stimmungen und seine Fragen. Die Erweckung der eigenen Erfahrung ist die Voraussetzung für jegliches Tasten und Ringen über sich hinaus.

Das Schweigen ist der Anfang des Fragens, die Leere ihr Grund. In sie hinein schwingt alles Bewegte und Gesehene aus. Auch die Zeit verlangsamt und dehnt sich hier.

Im Schweigen taucht der Mensch in seinen Grund ein und sucht Stand im «ewigen Jetzt». Der leere, sakrale Raum gewährt hier – mitten in derart gefüllter Zeit – Einkehr und Halt. Er legt den Weg aus, auf dem sich die Frage als Sein entfaltet. Es ist die Frage als Frage. Auch sie gehört wie das Schweigen fundamental zum menschlichen Leben selbst. Nur wenn der Mensch sich selber fraglich wird, wenn er in sich hineinblickt und sich von sich selbst erlöst, kann er sich verstehen: an seinem Ort in Raum und Zeit, in der Frage nach sich selbst und in der nach seiner Freiheit. Der Mensch stellt Fragen, ohne sie auszusprechen. Er kann sie nicht umgehen, denn sein Leben selbst ist die Frage.

Die Räume solcher Fragen werden im Film geöffnet. Peter Zumthor öffnet gleich zwei, die Feldkapelle und das Kolumba Museum. Mit der Kapelle öffnet er eine Schwellensituation. Er spricht von Räumen, die uns Schutz geben und gleichzeitig ein Gefühl von Weite schaffen. So entstehe eine Entgrenzung, eine Ahnung für das Endlose. Zumthors kleines Gotteshaus entspricht seiner Vorstellung von einem meditativen Raum, in dem man auf sich selber zurückgeworfen wird.

Der andere Raum ist das grosse Kolumba Museum in Köln. Es steht auf dem Ruinenfeld der alten Pfarrkirche zur heiligen Kolumba, ein Ort, beladener mit Geschichte. Zumthor bringt sie zum Sprechen mit einer hohen Überdachung. Er inszeniert sie sehr emotional, die Rekonstruktion des Bauwerks in einem eigenen Licht. In Gottes Licht? In mystischem Licht?

Das Nebeneinander von beidem, Mystik und Fragen, ist der Kern aller Energien für das Leben – und bleibt doch in den Gewissheiten schwankend. Im ständigen Wechsel von Frage und Antwort, eingespannt zwischen Wissen und Glauben, dauernd gebrochen im Zweifel, konturiert der Mensch die innere Evidenz des Letzten, sucht sie in gefüllter Einkehr, im Schweigen und in wortlosen Fragen wach zu halten. Doch findet er zu solchen Atmosphären?

Schon leuchten im Film die weissen Wände der Kirche Santa Maria in Marco de Canaveses im Norden Portugals auf. Sie stammt von Álvaro Siza Vieira. Aus dem Off hört man, wie sich der Raum als klare Begrenzung aufzulösen scheint. Versucht der Architekt hier das Unendliche spürbar zu machen?

Er spricht in seiner Muttersprache von den Erinnerungen an seine Kindheit, von seiner katholischen Erziehung, der Sonntagsmesse mit der Familie, der prägend geheimnisvollen Kirche in Matosinhos, seinem Geburtsort.

Was ihn als Kind faszinierte, waren die hohen Fenster seiner Heimatkirche. Später trat zu den eigenen Fragen etwas Neues hinzu, die eigene Gestaltung. Sie führte zu den weissen Kirchen, die das Werk bestimmen sollten, die offenen Plätze und die Innenräume mit ihren geradezu schwebenden Wänden.

Andere Wege ist Peter Märkli gegangen. Schon vor seinen Reisen von Burgund an den Atlantik entdeckte er die romanischen Kirchen in der Saintonge, ihre Geschichte und Masse und Grammatik; ihr Sein in der Zeit, vom Aufriss zum ständigen Weiterbau bis zur Umkehr – in Einbruch, Ruinen, Brocken und Sand. Erde zu Erde, Asche zu Asche. Doch was er im Sinn hatte – der Weg über Proportionen zum Rhythmus, vom Bauen mit Steinen zu den Tönen und Gesetzen der Musik! Die eigene Grammatik der Architektur führte ihn auf seinen eigenen Weg von der Archaik ins Innere der Welt, ins Jetzt und Heute.

Wir erfahren, wie dieser Architekt mit seinem Projekt von einer Zeit in die andere wandert. Das Ergebnis ist keine Kirche, es ist ein Raum, in dem Kunst ausgestellt wird. Aber es ist auch kein Museum. Es ist einfach ein Raum, virtuos verzweigt – eigens entstanden für die dauerhafte Präsentation vieler in sich ruhender Figuren von Hans Josephsohn. Geballte Statik, dynamisiert von einem «Architekten der Zeit», vom Jazz-Schlagzeuger Jojo Mayer. Seine Performance lässt die Wände tanzen, erregt den Raum, emotionalisiert die Skulpturen, überführt das Sehen der Augen in massloses Staunen und in Farben, die man nur ganz persönlich sehen kann.

Dieser Film konzentriert seine Bilder nicht auf die Dokumentation von Architektur, sondern offenbart seine Räume als schwebende Visualisierungen von Atmosphären. In sehr mattem, fast schon verlöschendem oder eben erst aufgehendem Licht zeigen sie sich im Ganzen, in Tiefenschärfe und feinsten Nuancen.

Was Christoph Schaub in seinem Film erzählt und was er untersucht, das bringen seine Bilder ans Licht, sie entdecken neue Räume, innere Bilder. Sie überführen die persönliche Erregung von Architekten, Künstlern und Musikern zu freien Assoziationen. So eröffnen sie Blicke für eine tiefe Nachdenklichkeit. Alles Erleben wird so gewissermassen spiegelnd wie spielerisch in die Eigenwelt des Betrachters überführt, ins Erinnern wie ins Fantasieren, ins Errichten seiner eigenen Binnenwelt. Damit sind Architektur, Kunst, Musik und Tanz bei ihrer eigenen Sache angekommen: das Sehen umzukehren, den Sehenden auf sich selbst zu verweisen und eigene, masslos sakrale Räume zu öffnen.

Speaking Spaces. Christoph Schaub's *Architecture of Infinity*

Friedhelm Mennekes

Artists like Eduardo Chillida (1924–2002) distinguish between geometric spaces and artistic spaces. The latter is the very thing that we as humans need in order to envision and discover ourselves. Each of us has to design, construct and furnish this space for ourselves. To begin with, this artistic space is a site where certain things appear: the volumes, the walls, and the objects that demarcate the space. Between and within these elements is emptiness. The formal purpose of the space is revealed by the activity of people, that is, by their intentional interaction with it.

Sacred space differs from this kind of artistic space – it is a hallowed site of reflection. I would like to mention three of its dimensions in terms of the functions of the space: it 'carries us away', it gathers, and it excites. Human beings need these kinds of sites – ones that offer a chance to escape the acoustic and visual noise of everyday life – and enter a space where silence reigns and where it is possible to truly listen and to experience one's inner reality. In this space, we can retreat within ourselves, in silent contemplation, and distance ourselves from the outside world.

In his new film about sacred spaces, Christoph Schaub uses a broad definition of architecture. Above all, he seeks to understand sacred spaces in terms of their effect, focusing his attention on the fascination that churches inspire in him. They appeal to him and interest him on an emotional

Friedhelm Mennekes is a Catholic theologian, priest, and art expert. He has written numerous books on questions of religion and art.

level because they speak to him personally.

Those who enter a church are seeking a state of peace. They want their emotions to settle and be absorbed by the atmosphere of the space. At first, visitors seek themselves, their story, their moods and their questions. The awakening of one's own experience is the precondition for any attempt – desperate or tentative – to reach beyond the self.

Silence is where questioning begins; emptiness its foundation. All emotion, all that we have seen enters into it and draws to a halt. Even time slows down and begins to stretch in this space. Enveloped by silence, we immerse ourselves in our foundations and seek a place in the 'eternal present'. The empty, sacred space grants reflection and relief – in the midst of such densely packed time. It lays out the path on which the question unfurls as existence. It is the question qua question. Like silence, it too fundamentally belongs to human life itself. It is only when we begin to question ourselves, when we glimpse inside and release us from ourselves that we can truly understand our own self: our position within time and space, the question of who we are and what makes us free. As humans, we pose questions without uttering them aloud. We cannot avoid them, because our life itself is the question.

The film opens up the spaces for such questions. Peter Zumthor opens two of them: the Feldkapelle and the Kolumba museum. With the Feldkapelle, he opens up a liminal space. He speaks of spaces that offer us protection and yet also create a feeling of expansiveness. Boundaries begin to dissolve and we gain a sense of the infinite. Zumthor's small house of God reflects his vision of a meditative space in which we are left alone with ourselves.

The other space is the large Kolumba museum in Cologne, which stands on the site of the ruins of the old St. Columba parish church – a site rich in history. With its high ceilings, Zumthor gives voice to this history, which he stages in a very emotive manner, positioning the reconstruction of the building in its own light. In God's light? In a mystical light?

The juxtaposition of both mysticism and questioning is the core of all of life's energies – and yet its certainties are always fluctuating. Constantly alternating between question and answer, caught between knowledge and faith, forever broken by doubt, the human being traces the inner evidence of finitude, seeks to keep it alive in active contemplation, in silence, and in wordless questions. But can we find our way to such an atmosphere?

In the film, the white walls of the Church of Santa Maria in Marco de Canaveses in the north of Portugal light up. The church is the work of Álvaro Siza Vieira. In the voiceover, we hear how the space's clear boundaries seem to dissolve. Is the architect trying to make the infinite tangible? He speaks in his native

tongue about memories of his childhood, of his Catholic upbringing, of Sunday Mass with the family, of the formatively mysterious church in Matosinhos, his birthplace.

What fascinated him as a child were the high windows of the church in his hometown. Later, he added something new to his questioning: his own design, which led to the white churches that would define the work, the open courtyards, and the interiors with their almost floating walls.

Peter Märkli took a different path. Even before he travelled from Burgundy to the Atlantic he had discovered the Romanesque churches of Saintonge, their history and mass, their formal grammar; their existence in time, from their design to the eternal continuation of their construction and their eventual return – collapsing into ruins, fragments and sand. Earth to earth, ashes to ashes. But what he had in mind – creating rhythm through proportions, progressing from building in stone to the sounds and laws of music! His personal architectural grammar led him on his own path from the archaic to the interior world, to the here and now.

We see how this architect wanders from one era to another with his project. The result is not a church but a space in which art is exhibited. Yet it is not a museum either. It is just a space, breathtakingly ramified, specifically created for the purpose of permanently presenting many of Hans Josephsohn's contemplative figures. Concentrated stasis, made dynamic by an 'architect of time', the jazz drummer Jojo Mayer. His performance makes the walls dance, excites the space, imbues the sculptures with emotion, converts what we see with our eyes into boundless amazement and colours that each person perceives individually.

This film does not limit its images to documenting architecture, but rather reveals the spaces it depicts as floating visualisations of atmospheres. In dull light that is almost fading away or only just beginning to emerge, they show themselves in their entirety, in high definition and finely nuanced.

What Christoph Schaub relays in his film and what he investigates is brought to light through his images, which discover new spaces, inner images. They transform the personal excitement of architects, artists and musicians into free association, opening glimpses into a deep form of contemplation. All experience is, as it were, mirrored, playfully transported into the personal world of the viewer, into memory and fantasy, into the construction of their own inner world. With this, architecture, art, music and dance arrive at their true purpose: to invert sight, to turn the gaze of the seer back on themselves, and to force them to open up their own limitlessly sacred spaces.

Der Endlichkeit ein Schnippchen schlagen
Ein Gespräch mit Christoph Schaub

Die Fragen stellten
Susanne Schnell und Louise Blättler

Was war Ihr Verständnis von Architektur bei Ihrem Film Architektur der Unendlichkeit?

Ich versuche, den Begriff der Architektur weit zu fassen, Architektur im Sinne der räumlichen Erfahrung universeller zu verstehen. Ich gehe im Film von Räumen mit sakraler Wirkung aus. Räume, die Erhabenheit, Überwältigung oder Schutz auslösen wollen. Diese Wirkung kann sich auch in einem profanen Gebäude, in der Natur oder in der Kunst entfalten. Die Architektur thematisiert das Thema der Unendlichkeit in einem sehr basalen Sinn, denn ein Gebäude schneidet ja einen Teil aus dem Unendlichen heraus. Architektur kann somit sinnbildlich für das Endliche im Unendlichen stehen. Kirchen beispielsweise thematisieren das Jenseits, als Gegenentwurf zum endlichen Leben auf der Erde. Heutzutage suchen wir Menschen in der Natur und in der Kunst eine ähnliche, (nicht-religiöse) Erfahrung – eine Erfahrung der Entrückung, vielleicht der Spiritualität.

Was haben Sie selbst erlebt und erfahren beim Machen dieses Films? Hat Sie das Machen dieses Filmes verändert?

Während der Arbeit hat sich bezüglich der Thematik vieles verändert, d.h. vor allem mein Interesse daran hat sich verändert. Ich habe entdeckt, dass ich nicht nur einen Film über sakrale Architektur mache, sondern auch, dass ich aus meinem Leben erzählen muss. Dadurch wurde mir bewusst, dass die eigentliche sakrale Architektur nie vorrangig im Mittelpunkt meines Interesses stand. Ich habe auch gemerkt, dass ich den Begriff des Raums ausweiten will und folglich auch über den Raum im Innern des Menschen nachdenken möchte. Erst dadurch kann ein Bild für eine Architektur der Unendlichkeit gefunden werden. Der innere Raum kann als unendlich betrachtet werden – jedenfalls hat er keine sichtbaren Grenzen, keinen Anfang, kein Ende und auch keinen Mittelpunkt, denn er ist eigentlich überall.

Nach welchen Kriterien haben Sie die Protagonisten und Bauwerke gewählt?

Mir waren zwei Dinge wichtig: Einerseits mussten die Protagonisten und Bauwerke in Bezug auf mein Erzählinteresse inspirierend wirken. Anderseits mussten sie zueinander passen. Hierbei habe ich mir immer vorgestellt, würden sich die Protagonisten bei gutem Wein und Essen treffen, dann müssten sie sich prächtig unterhalten, sich mögen und einander respektieren – kurz: Sie sollten einen inspirierenden Abend miteinander verbringen.

Wie inszeniert man Raum in einem Film, damit er für den Zuschauer lebendig wird?

Ich glaube nicht, dass man den Raum einfach realistisch abbilden kann. Sondern man muss einen emotionalen Zugang finden; den Raum emotional erzählen. Das ist dann in diesem Sinn nicht mehr realistisch. Es beginnt schon damit, dass der Film zweidimensional und das Erlebnis dreidimensional ist. Es gilt also, Ersatz zu schaffen, und um dies zu erreichen, hat man zahlreiche Möglichkeiten: Licht, Ton, Musik. Aber auch die Wahl, wie man einen Raum in der Montage zusammensetzt. Mir war es ein Anliegen, dass die Räume im Film als emotionale Erfahrung erlebt werden.

Die Paraglider, brechenden Wellen und Sternenbilder im Film symbolisieren die Unendlichkeit des Raums. Für was stehen die spielenden Kinder, die Sie zeigen?

Mit den Kindern beginnt der Film, weil Kinder in einem gewissen Sinn elementar sind: Sie buddeln Löcher und bauen mit Leintüchern häufig Hütten oder Ähnliches. Ich spreche natürlich auch von mir. Das ist so eine Anfangsenergie, auch in Bezug auf Architektur: Etwas bauen, etwas Endliches im Unendlichen erschaffen. Im Film geht es ja auch um die Endlichkeit und den Tod. Was kommt danach? Was ist vor dem Anfang? Was ist nach dem Ende? Kinder sind frei von diesen Fragen. Sie sind in der Lage, einen anderen Bezug zur Welt zu schaffen: Eine Art Reise, einen Rückzug nach innen zu durchleben. Die Kinderszenen im Film verstehe ich als eine Traumebene, die dem «Rationalen» gegenübersteht. Zudem sind die Kinder ein schöner Kontrast zu den in die Jahre gekommenen Protagonisten.

Was waren bei diesem Film die grössten künstlerischen Herausforderungen für Sie?

Eine wesentliche Herausforderung war es, die verschiedenen Ebenen des Films in ein interessantes Verhältnis zu setzen. Auf der Bildebene denke ich hier vor allem an die Interaktion zwischen der Erzählung der Architektur und der Landschaften, die naturgegeben eher statisch und, man könnte fast sagen: objektiv ist, und der «inneren» Bilder, die bewegter und natürlich subjektiver sind. Auf der Tonebene war das Zusammenspiel von Sounddesign und Jojo Mayers Musik herausfordernd. Schliesslich galt es, eine Off-Erzählung zu finden, die persönlich ist und gleichzeitig auch an gewissen Stellen informativ. Wir haben immer gesagt, die Off-Erzählung muss bei der Zuschauerin etwas «triggern» – ein Interesse, eine Emotion oder eine Erinnerung. Letztlich könnte ich die Frage auch so beantworten: Es ging darum, dem Bildkünstler Ramon Giger, der Schnittkünstlerin Marina Wernli und dem Musikkünstler Jojo Mayer ein produktives Vis-à-vis und ein «Inspirator» zu sein.

Wie müsste die Kirche aussehen, die Sie bauen würden?

Ich bin ja kein Architekt. Ich kann nur sagen, im Skyspace in Zuoz habe ich mir gedacht, so müsste eine Kirche sein – vom räumlichen Empfinden her und von dem, was mit einem passiert dort drinnen. Der Skyspace hat die Form eines Zylinders und ist daher nicht zentralperspektivisch wie viele andere Kirchen. In der Decke gibt es eine runde Aussparung, durch die man in den Himmel schauen kann. James Turrell hat zudem im Innenraum eine raffinierte Lichtshow eingebaut, die bei mir ein Gefühl des Schwebens auslöste.

Ziemlich anders als konventionelle Kirchen …

Die Kirchen repräsentieren immer auch die Institution, die Autorität. Eine Kirche kann einen als Individuum in diesem Sinne nicht befreien, sondern sie richtet. Die Kunst aber trägt in sich den Auftrag, den Menschen zu befreien; freie Räume zu schaffen, im Innern des Menschen. Darum finde ich den Skyspace von Turrell so genial: weil er einen schützt und gleichzeitig Freiraum gibt. Es ist ein Kunstprojekt – man fühlt sich frei. Ich habe dort diese Spannung stark erlebt, es gibt auf der einen Seite einen Schutz und Grenzen und auf der anderen Seite Freiheit. Die Spannung zwischen diesen beiden Polen finde ich extrem wichtig für das Leben. Um Ihre vorhergehende Frage zu beantworten: Ich würde versuchen, in diese Richtung zu gehen: einen Raum zu schaffen, der gleichzeitig Schutz und Freiheit gibt.

Ist dieser Film Ihr persönlichster Dokumentarfilm?

Ja, dies ist mein «persönlichster» Film, in dem Sinne, dass die Erzählung von meinen Interessen, meinen Erfahrungen und Gefühlen bestimmt wird. Es war mir jedoch wichtig, dass der Film gleichzeitig Erfahrungen und Gefühle vieler Menschen reflektiert. Der Zugang soll universell sein und auf keinen Fall unpersönlich. Die Ebene der Ich-Erzählung half mir, dieses Gleichgewicht zu finden.

Eine meiner Lieblingsszenen ist die mit Álvaro Siza: Jeden Morgen übermalt er die Warnhinweise auf seiner Zigarettenschachtel mit einer Zeichnung.

Für mich ist es seine Rebellion gegen die Endlichkeit – was ist es für Sie?

Für mich auch! Darum ist die Szene auch im Film. Ich habe die Zeichnung auf der Zigarettenschachtel gesehen und ihn spontan danach gefragt. Und dann hat Siza mir genau das Richtige dazu gesagt. Sie haben Recht, das ist, mit einem Augenzwinkern, seine Rebellion. Er will der Endlichkeit ein Schnippchen schlagen.

Cheating Finitude

A conversation with Christoph Schaub

Questions posed by
Susanne Schnell and Louise Blättler

What was your concept of architecture in your film Architecture of Infinity?

I try to define the concept of architecture broadly, to understand architecture more universally in the sense of spatial experience. In the film, I begin with spaces that have a sacred effect; spaces that seek to trigger a sense of the sublime, of protection, or that seek to overwhelm. This effect can also develop in a secular building, in nature or in art. Architecture deals with the issue of infinity in a very fundamental sense, because a building carves a little piece out of the infinite. Architecture can therefore symbolise the finite in the infinite. Churches, for example, speak to the afterlife as an alternative to this finite life on earth. These days, we humans seek a similar (non-religious) experience in nature and in art – an experience of rapture, perhaps of spirituality.

What did you experience and discover while making this film? Did making this film change you?

While I was working, a lot changed in terms of the subject matter – that is to say, more than anything, my interest in it changed. I discovered that I was not just making a film about sacred architecture, but that I would also have to tell stories from my own life. So it became clear to me that sacred architecture itself was never my primary interest. I also realised that I wanted to expand the concept of what a space is and, consequently, I also wanted to think about the space within human beings. That's the only way that an

image of an architecture of infinity can be found. Inner spaces can be considered infinite – well, they certainly don't have visible boundaries, no beginning, no end and also no centre, because ultimately, they are everywhere.

What were your criteria for selecting the protagonists and the buildings?

Two things were important to me. On the one hand, the protagonists and buildings had to be inspiring in terms of my narrative interest. On the other hand, they had to fit together well. While I was choosing them, I would always imagine that if the protagonists were to meet for a glass of wine and a good meal, then they would have to have a great conversation, to like and respect one another. In short: they would have an inspiring evening together.

How do you stage a space in a film so that it comes to life for the viewer?

I don't believe that you can simply depict space realistically. Rather, you have to find a point of emotional connection; you have to narrate the space on an emotional level. Which means that it then essentially ceases to be realistic. And that begins with the fact that films are two-dimensional and experience is three-dimensional. So it's a matter of creating replacements, and there are many ways to achieve that: light, sound, music. But also the choice of how the space is put together in the montage. It was important to me that the viewer experience the spaces in the film emotionally.

The paragliders, breaking waves and constellations in the film symbolise the infinite nature of space. What do the playing children in your film represent?

The film begins with children because children are, in a certain sense, elemental. They dig holes and build forts and the like with bed sheets. I am also speaking about myself here, of course. It's such a primeval energy, also with regard to architecture: to build something, to create something finite within the infinite. The film also deals with mortality and death. What comes after? What is before the beginning? What is after the end? Children aren't troubled by these questions. They are capable of forging a different connection with the world; to go through a kind of journey, they can withdraw into themselves. I understand the scenes in the film that involve children as a kind of dreamscape that stands in opposition to the 'rational'. Also, the children provide a nice contrast to the ageing protagonists.

What were the greatest artistic challenges you encountered when making this film?

It was a considerable challenge to find an interesting way to relate the different levels of the film to one another. On the visual level, I'm thinking here above all about the interaction between the narration of the architecture and the landscapes, which is naturally more static, and, you could almost say, objective, and the 'internal' images, which are more animated, and of course more subjective. In terms of the soundtrack, the interplay between the sound design and Jojo Mayer's music was challenging. Finally, it was important to find a voice-over narration that was personal but also informative at certain points. We always said that the narration had to 'trigger' something in the viewer – an interest, an emotion, or a memory. Ultimately, I could also answer this question by saying that my role was about providing the visual artist Ramon Giger, the editor Marina Wernli and the musician Jojo Mayer with a productive counterpart, to inspire them.

If you were to build a church, what would it look like?

I mean, I'm not an architect. I can only say that when I was in Skyspace in Zuoz, I thought, this is what a church should be like – in terms of the spatial feel and what happens to you when you're inside it. Skyspace is shaped like a cylinder, which means it has no linear perspective, like most other churches. There is a circular opening in the ceiling through which you can look at the sky. Also, James Turrell has installed a sophisticated light show in the interior which made me feel as if I were floating.

Quite a change from conventional churches ...

Churches always also represent the institution, authority. In this sense, a church cannot liberate a person as an individual, rather, it directs them. But the mission of art is to liberate humankind, to create free spaces within people. That's why I find Turrell's Skyspace so ingenious: because it protects you while at the same time giving you freedom. It's an art project – you feel free. That tension was really present for me when I was there. On the one hand, it gives you protection and boundaries, and on the other hand, freedom. I consider the tension between these two poles to be extremely important in life. To answer your previous question though, that would be the direction I would want to go in: to create a space that simultaneously provides both protection and freedom.

Is this film your most personal documentary film?

Yes, this is my 'most personal' film in the sense that the narration is determined by my interests, my experiences and my feelings. But it was important to me that the film also reflect the experiences and feelings of a whole range of people. It should be universally accessible and definitely not impersonal. The use of first-person narration helped me to strike this balance.

One of my favourite scenes is the one with Álvaro Siza: every morning he covers the warning label on his pack of cigarettes with a drawing. For me, this act is his rebellion against the finitude of life – how do you interpret it?

Me too! That's why the scene is in the film. I saw the drawing on the cigarette pack and immediately asked him about it. And Siza's answer was perfect. And you're right – in a playful way, that's his rebellion. He wants to cheat finitude a little.

Peter Zumthor

Architekt/Architect, Haldenstein, CH

Geboren 1943. Ausbildung als Möbelschreiner. Studium der Innenarchitektur, Design und Architektur an der Kunstgewerbeschule Basel und am Pratt Institute in New York. Seit 1978 eigenes Architekturbüro in Haldenstein (GR). Peter Zumthor hat zahlreiche Architekturpreise erhalten, u.a. den Pritzker Preis.

Born in 1943. Joiner's apprenticeship. Studied Interior Architecture, Design and Architecture at the Basel School for Applied Arts and at the Pratt Institute in New York. In 1978, he set up his own architectural firm in Haldenstein (Canton of Graubünden, CH). Peter Zumthor has received numerous architecture awards, including the Pritzker Architecture Prize.

Álvaro Siza Vieira

Architekt/Architect, Porto, PT

Geboren 1933. Lebt und arbeitet in Porto und betreibt seit 1958 sein Architekturbüro. In Portugal gilt Siza als Hauptvertreter der Moderne. Für sein Werk erhielt er zahlreiche wichtige Auszeichnungen, u.a. den Pritzker Preis.

Born in 1933. Lives and works in Porto, where he founded his architectural firm in 1958. Siza is considered to be Portugal's main representative of Modernist architecture. He has received numerous important distinctions for his work, including the Pritzker Architecture Prize.

Jojo Mayer

Musiker, Schlagzeuger/Musician, drummer, New York, USA

Geboren 1963. Ein in New York lebender Schweizer Schlagzeuger, der unter anderem mit Jazzgrössen wie Dizzy Gillespie, Nina Simone und John Zorn arbeitete. Hat seine eigene Band NERVE.

Born in 1963. A Swiss drummer residing in New York, who has worked with jazz greats such as Dizzy Gillespie, Nina Simone and John Zorn. He has his own band called NERVE.

Cristina Iglesias

Künstlerin/Artist, Madrid, ES

Geboren 1956. Eine spanische Installationskünstlerin und Bildhauerin, die in Torrelodones, Madrid lebt und arbeitet. Sie arbeitet mit vielen Materialien, darunter Stahl, Wasser, Glas, Bronze, Bambus, Stroh.

Born in 1956. A Spanish installation artist and sculptor, who lives and works in Torrelodones, Madrid. Her work is comprised of a variety of materials, including steel, water, glass, bronze, bamboo and straw.

James Turrell

Künstler/Artist, Flagstaff, USA

Geboren 1943. Der wichtigste amerikanische Land-Art- und Licht-Künstler. Er setzt sich in seinem reichen Schaffen hauptsächlich mit dem Verhältnis von Raum und Licht auseinander.

Born in 1943. The most prominent Land Art and Light artist in the U.S. His rich body of work predominantly deals with the relationship between space and light.

Peter Märkli

Architekt/Architect, Zürich, CH

Geboren 1953. Studium an der ETH Zürich. Von 2002–2015 bekleidet er eine Professur an der ETH Zürich. Seit 2013 Visiting Professor an der MARCH School of Architecture in Moskau. Er führt sein eigenes Büro in Zürich.

Born in 1953. Studied at the ETH in Zurich. From 2002 to 2015, he was a professor at ETH Zurich. Since 2013, Visiting Professor at the MARCH School of Architecture in Moscow. He runs his own architectural firm in Zurich.

Christoph Schaub

Regisseur/Director, Zürich, CH

Geboren 1958 in Zürich, brach das Germanistikstudium zugunsten seiner filmischen Aktivitäten ab. Innerhalb der Zürcher Jugendbewegung der 80er-Jahre entstanden seine ersten Filme. 1987 realisierte Christoph Schaub seinen ersten Spielfilm – *Wendel.* Heute besteht sein filmisches Werk aus insgesamt 12 Spielfilmen und 16 Dokumentarfilmen in verschiedenen Formaten.

Ein grösseres Kinopublikum kennt ihn als Regisseur erfolgreicher Spielfilme wie *Giulias Verschwinden, Jeune Homme* oder *Sternenberg.* Ein wichtiger Teil seines Schaffens sind jedoch auch die Dokumentarfilme zu architektonischen und urbanistischen Themen.

Christoph Schaub ist Mitglied der Schweizer Filmakademie, der European Film Academy (EFA) und der Asian Pacific Screen Academy. Seine Filme erhalten national wie international grosse Aufmerksamkeit und Anerkennung.

Born 1958 in Zurich, quit his studies of German to follow his interest in filming. He created his first films in and around the Zurich youth movement of the 1980s. Christoph Schaub realised his first own feature film titled *Wendel* in 1987. Today, his cinematic work comprises 10 feature films and 16 documentaries of different formats.

He is known to a larger cinema audience as the director of successful movies such as *Giulias Verschwinden, Happy New Year, Jeune Homme,* or *Sternenberg.* Documentaries on architecture and urbanistic topics, however, constitute another important part of his creative work.

Christoph Schaub is a member of the Swiss Film Academy, the European Film Academy (EFA), and the Asian Pacific Screen Academy. His films receive broad attention and are celebrated both nationally and worldwide.

www.schaubfilm.ch